'twas ever thus

'twas ever thus

A selection of Eastern Canadian Folk Art

Foreword by Joan Murray
Preface by Ralph and Patricia Price
Introduction by J. Russell Harper

M. F. Feheley Publishers

© 1979 M. F. Feheley Publishers
5 Drumsnab Road, Toronto, Canada

ISBN: 0-919880-15-0 (Softbound)
0-919880-16-9 (Hardbound)

ISBN: 0-919880-15-0 (Softbound)
0-919880-16-9 (Hardbound)

Printed and bound in Canada

Contents ✑

Foreword

Folk art is a considerably neglected aspect of our culture. For this reason, it is fortunate for all of us that for the past twelve years Ralph and Patricia Price have collected with sensitivity and integrity the work of these little known artists. These two dynamic people have an acute understanding of our heritage and all its historical complexities, and this knowledge is reflected in their collection.

Folk art is so vigorous and dynamic that it is hard to define. In general, its essence is spontaniety; the work may also be considered naïve, primitive or regional. Certain contemporary artists, like Tony Urquhart and Joyce Wieland, have said to me that they are folk artists because they work in a manner similar to the "grass roots" artists; it's a comparison worth thinking about while reading the Price's Preface and J. Russell Harper's Introduction to *'Twas Ever Thus,* or while viewing the collection.

Originally, our specific intent in organizing an exhibition of the Price Collection was to reveal that in Port Perry, in the Region of Durham, there is a collection — and a major one in Canada — of this material. As well, we wished to point out the significance of the facts that this collection is fully documented and is formed totally of Canadian works.

As a regional gallery, we were interested in what is particularly different about our area. But this collection provides us with more than a regional insight; it is a contribution to the history of Canadian art. *'Twas Ever Thus* is a record and an explanation of this important contribution.

Joan Murray
Director
The Robert McLaughlin Gallery
Oshawa, Ontario

Preface

What has become a collection of eastern Canadian folk art grew from a fairly typical beginning: a collection of Canadian country antiques. Our first pieces of early Canadian furniture were acquired from necessity; we had an empty house, and we needed furniture. Our funds were limited.

For whatever reasons, external or internal, the acquisitive character of the collector emerges, the climate or chemistry in our case must have been right. Our brush with early furniture had made a marked impression. It had, in fact, ignited a fire. We had become collectors, insatiable collectors with catholic tastes.

Initially furniture collectors, with a small side interest in early tools, we began to selectively acquire those decorative accessories which would have found daily use alongside our furniture: the butter prints, the quilts, the rugs and the decorated stoneware.

About 1968, two years into our collecting habit — our new lifestyle — we paid a visit to the Farmer's Museum at Cooperstown, New York. Across the road is Fennimore House where we viewed the magnificent collection of folk art on display. It was probably about this time we realized that our collection of furnishings contained the nucleus of a folk art collection. We purchased books on the subject, we read magazine articles, our interest and excitement grew. We discovered contemporary folk art, and our collection broadened. It is still broadening. What is shown here is our collection at this time. It is, however, a dynamic, growing thing. This is not an end point. Rather, it is an important roadmark. It is that time at which we declare ourselves and publicly air our collecting eccentricities. The collection is subject to valid criticism, it has certain gaps, but that does not make it less exciting. It is an eclectic collection, certainly, and any of the pieces within it could be adequately replaced by a number of other extant pieces. Instead of being a criticism of the collection, this is a testimonial to the body of works that is Canadian folk art; its variety, its richness. Because of the great range of expression, organization has become a problem, and what follows outlines a workable plan to bring order out of chaos.

The great variety of expressions that are classified as folk art present one of the major problems in understanding it as a whole. This large, "acceptable" grouping has come about through various means, not the least of which is confusion. This confusion is not only over what is acceptable as folk art, but if indeed folk art itself is acceptable as a designation. The weathervane is a good example to use in exploring this acceptable versus unacceptable situation. Few would quarrel with the designation of a tinsmith's individual interpretation of the running horse weathervane as folk art. However, the factory produced running horse, the product of small operations, such as the Pedlar People in Oshawa, are to some less acceptable.

In such cases, it would appear that individual artistic expression as opposed to the directed expression of the manufacturing process is the watershed or dividing line. Nevertheless, many pieces which were in effect factory made have been called folk art for many years. These include sophisticated weathervanes, the trade figures made to order, and others. These have been lumped together with the obviously handmade category that includes carved toys, primitive paintings, certain decoys, and so on.

Personally, we accept them all as folk art, accept them all as valid folk expressions. However, their diversity requires that some sort of organization be imposed to bring order out of confusion. Probably the best device we have discovered for putting individual pieces into a manageable order is the "circle system" which was devised by Louis C. and Agnes Halsey Jones of the New York State Historical Association at Cooperstown. It is currently called *Tentative Version Number Three.*

The word "tentative" in this title is very significant, and it is typical of the Jones' openmindedness to new ideas. Both its title and contents urge personal involvement; this is not the definitive circle, but it does have the benefit of organizing folk art into a manageable whole. It is used here, somewhat altered to fit our collection and the Canadian situation, with the kind permission of the inventors.

The inner circle of this aid to the classification of folk art is called "Traditional Folk Art," and it contains those pieces in which the individual artistic expression of the creator is evident. A good example of a piece that belongs in this category is *The Yellow Band,* a powerful piece of folk sculpture made about 1975 by George Cockayne, a farmer from the Madoc area of Ontario. Why he chose this particular form is uncertain, but he admits to "reading a lot — mostly magazines." Perhaps his inspiration and model came from the pages of the *National Geographic* or some similar publication. In any case, it appears to be a unique and highly individual piece of folk sculpture.

The outer circle, "Associative Folk Art," is more contentious and contains those pieces which have evident artistic expression but of a sort that is less individual and more channelled or directed. So-called school-taught arts, such as calligraphy, are good examples. The products of cottage industries or small factories also fall into this category, because their direction comes from a teacher or shop management. Although such figures as *Alice the Cigar Store Indian Maiden* have generally been accepted as folk art, they were the products of relatively sophisticated shops that made them to order.

Alice was named for a Micmac Indian woman who sold baskets in Charlottetown at the turn of the century; the figure stood in the Riley Tobacco Company in Charlottetown throughout the last quarter of the nineteenth century. Possibly locally made but probably not, she appears to be the made-to-order product of a sophisticated carver who worked in a shop setting.

Problems arise in any classification system, and this particular one is no different. Some pieces of folk art that we might place in the inner circle may well be put in the outer one by others and vice versa. In many cases, the assignment of a group to both circles at the same time will tend to confuse rather than clarify the issue. The essence is the difference between individual work and that which has been supervised; the individual, hand carved decoy as opposed to the factory version.

Of course, if we knew the individual artist or artisan responsible for each piece, knew his artistic intentions, and more of his models and methods of production, then circle assignment could be much more confidently done. This lack of knowledge is primarily the case with nineteenth century pieces, a disadvantage that is tempered by what we know of contemporary folk artists and their work. One can often

Associative Folk Art
(Directed Work)

School Taught Arts: theorems, memorials, calligraphy and needle arts.

Traditional Folk Art
(Individual Work)

Sculpture (all sizes and media), paintings, textiles (quilts, samplers and hooked rugs), weathervanes, whirlygigs, toys, decoys, trade signs, butterprints, sugar moulds, environmentals, grave markers, decorated wrought iron, painted walls, fireboards, potter's whimsies.

More recently, decorated vans and decorated denim.

Products of cottage industry, small factories or shops: trade figures, figureheads, weathervanes, decorated stoneware, butterprints, decoys, carousel figures

Work which is close to a "Craft Tradition": feather and hair wreaths, hooked rugs (pattern), samplers (pattern), paintings after prints, ethnic art (ie. Ukranian Easter eggs), food traditions.

Introduction

The Price Collection of Folk Art excites the eye, lifts the spirit and touches the heart. It is a collection of art objects made by ordinary folk and designed to appeal to those in the little places. They were created in order to make the daily routine richer, while at the same time they reflect historic roots and the inner life of those who made them. They appeal to the kindly individual moved by emotional appeal rather than the power of the market place.

The collection is bewildering in its diversity; there are articles of wood, metal and fabric. They have been assembled in twelve short years from many places by Dr. Ralph Price and his wife Patricia. These two collectors have eagerly combed the many byways in search of the visually stimulating; those things that the simple artist has enriched visually; things that strike chords of pleasure in their owners as they did for those who displayed them in the past. Their search has taken the Prices over much of southern Ontario. They have hunted through the old French-speaking villages and farmlands bordering the St. Lawrence. They have travelled further and found carvings, nostalgic models and household articles of beauty and interest dating from both early and more recent years in New Brunswick, Nova Scotia and Prince Edward Island. Indeed, their treks have taken them to those areas that embraced the original Canadian heartland. The Prices have covered the bounds envisioned by Macdonald, Cartier, Tilley, Tupper and Gray as encompassing early Confederation.

There is no easy definition of the term "folk art" as seen in the Price Collection. A folk object is one overlaid with the decorative or artistic touches of a sensitive craftsman and intended for the humbler homes, a setting where it will be enjoyed for its own sake. The decorative pattern added to a trivet (No. 18) by the local blacksmith is such a folk expression, for it transforms a purely utilitarian piece into an artistic article. Untrained but intuitive and gifted painters who set down records of their surroundings, their fantasies or portraits of their friends are folk painters. Equally, the man who carves decorations on a handmade box (No. 9) in order to please the eye is a folk carver by taking the form beyond the mundane and utilitarian.

Folk objects reflect both an inner artistic and an aesthetic sense. The Price Collection would be described more precisely as one of "vernacular" art, because it corresponds to the plain speech of plain people in places away from the mainstream whose language is overlaid by colourful local sayings, quiet humour and twists of pronunciation that develop on the sideroads. To call this a collection of folk art is to give a peculiarly North American interpretation to the expression. European peasant people have taken centuries to develop traditional art forms in dress, national allegiances, religious beliefs and local superstitions. Canadian society is neither homogenous enough in our multi-cultured mosaic, nor is it sufficiently old to have resolved itself into distinct expressions. On the other hand, these Canadian objects are made by uninhibited and lively workers who have spent long winter evenings in rural or side street environments; they have an urge to create, and what they have created speaks loudly of Canada, of personal roots and of the personal spirit of its people.

One ponders the origins and motivations of this "art". An elderly lady once described how her grandfather sat by a fireplace in the pioneer Glengarry County of eastern Ontario. There he whittled like many other "whittlers" in those parts. Mostly he simply pared away long white pine slivers that curled and floated to the floor like graceful feathers; there they were collected to light his pipe during hours of contemplative smoking. But he was aware of his grandchildren, and with the affection of a grandparent carved out with naïve imagination animals marching two by two into Noah's ark. This same humility and lively spirit inspired Silas Brokenshire of Fenelon Falls, Ontario, in 1890 to fashion a rocking horse (No. 38) for his son Foster. Silas made pumps for his pioneer neighbours. The horse was rugged and chunky like the tough little work horses of the small farms. It would have been completely out of character to carve a purebred gentleman's pacer. Yet the son's horse has a rugged beauty, and it mirrors a love that transforms it into a superb object when viewed as folk art. It also symbolizes human pathos; Foster died at the age of five as did many small children in the 19th century.

The objects in the Price Collection are really an open window to see the inner nature of their makers. It is a fascinating view. The earlier folk art of Victorian Ontario has a widespread communal ethos, while that of more recent years is more personal and diverse. It is worthwhile to take a closer look at the Ontario scene as one part of the folk art spectrum, particularly because Canadian folk art has a different spirit when one travels from region to region. The overtones of well-being of the Ontario farm people, their appreciation of subtle beauty and their pride of achievement astonishes those who examine the quilts of the 19th century in the Price Collection. One has an appliquéd *Rose of Sharon* design (No. 55). This is a traditional pattern but one that is overlaid here with a personal touch in the choice of rose hues that are arresting in their harmonious beauty. The calm and

ordered scrolls of the design sooth the soul, exude well-being and are executed with incredible craftsmanship. Equally, there is another quilt of great artistic merit into which the maker has poured hours and hours of labour. In this example, a myriad of triangular patches of fragile, coloured fabric have been cunningly arranged and pieced together like a mosaic in a grid pattern of light and dark hues; the strong geometric forms have the solid strength of barn frames raised at traditional "bees". Edith May Prout of Zephyr, Ontario made a patchwork quilt of homespun in the late 19th century combining red crosses and whirling yellow swastikas on green squares (No. 57). Its lively hues delight. That she used harsh homespun seems particularly appropriate, for her family had struggled through such harsh pioneer conditions that in respect their neighbours referred to them as living on "Prout's Road".

This was a time when exotic, decorative theorem paintings (No. 43) added colour to the wall, perhaps with a bright spot of pheasants. Hooked mats were equally exotic notes. They were becoming fashionable, and the basic form gave unlimited scope to the folk artist. The earliest dated example in Canada was made near Fredericton, New Brunswick, in 1860. With obvious satisfaction, it renders a new and neat little house in suburban New Maryland. Ontario women were doing the same, and examples in the Price Collection follow this old tradition but also include a fantistic lion (No. 49). There is also one (No. 48) with a large black rooster traced from a weathervane by Mrs. Crozier of Lennox and Addington County; with its yellow feet, yellow border and Scotch thistles in each corner, it caught the eye of all that came into the living room. One of the most exciting examples of this particular expression of folk expression is a pair of mats (Nos. 52 & 53) depicting the kings and queens of the card deck. These mats, created by Flora Christie of Manchester, Ontario, are of a later date than the New Brunswick example, but they retain the older creative spirit, while doing homage to the playing cards that provided innumerable evenings of amusement for the family circle.

There are those folk carvers in Ontario who expressed national loyalties and satisfaction with their Canada through ornamental signs that enlivened the village street. On the shop of an Oshawa music dealer was a carved and painted beaver (No. 58), doubtless meant as a patriotic symbol during the years when Sir Sanford Fleming had placed a beaver on the country's first postage stamp. The music shop also must have sold the song "The Maple Leaf Forever" which became a traditional Canadian folk song, chanted in every little red school house up and down Ontario. The beaver was proverbially and repeatedly used to proclaim a belief in the virtue of industry. Hence, this little animal won a place both on Montreal's coat of arms and on those of other places. It ornamented, for example, the barn roof of a prosperous farm belonging to a man from Omemee, Ontario (No. 6).

This was a time of stability with hard work on the one side of the scale balanced in happy equilibrium by the fruits of that labour on the other. Waterloo County, with its Ontario German Mennonite community, had a long history of hard work, respect for church and fellow man, and quickly achieved a state of independence not unlike that of other farm communities in the province. Theirs was a quiet atmosphere, one that fostered the continuance of the ancient folk art

traditions they had brought with them as well as giving birth to new forms of expression. The collection includes a flax hackle (No. 20) used by Waterloo County Mennonite pioneers in the laborious first steps in making linen. This piece is mounted on a softly polished board which has been decorated with simply curved edges and elaborated with restrained concentric circles. Such simple design is appropriate to a people who practice frugality and have done so for centuries. Even more subtly restrained is a simple cabbage shredder (No. 21) used in the making of traditional sauerkraut. A simple implement, yet it is made to hang neatly on the wall with a heart-shaped hole drilled through a wooden scallop and with an echoing decorative void at the other end, a quality that reflects gentle satisfaction, contentment and "niceness".

A little wooden mallet is one of the most unusual expressions of good will that one will find in folk art. Edwin Willis made it about 1880 (No. 33). He polished it with such care that it must have been made to admire and never to crack the walnuts that grew on the trees down the road. Newmarket, where Willis lived, was one of those towns in Ontario where peace-loving Quakers settled and where life was calm and peaceful. It can be no mere coincidence that he chose to decorate his mallet with an engraved dove holding an olive branch. Willis had lived a good life and had a kindly feeling for his neighbours, yet he, like every other man in the village, played a definite role and felt himself an integral part of the overall scheme of things. He was no nameless assembly-line robot so he boldly engraved his name below the bird. The decorative motif is copied from a Spencerian script copy book. This was one of those aids purchased by our forefathers to improve their penmanship. Writing was then an art, and elegantly written letters to friends or neat rows of figures in ledgers had a certain beauty and were sources of pride. They had a definite aesthetic quality, in much the same way that Chinese calligraphers still regard written mottos and inscriptions.

The immigrant who came to Canada found that by the Confederation years his life had been transformed and he had become a minor squire. It had been done by hard work. Out of the earlier drudgery of clearing the primeval forest, came the ability to provide food and shelter for himself and his family. He was optimistic about the future, and he was at peace with his church, his neighbours and his country. It was a time of well-being that demanded artistic and other warming touches that would transform simple shelter into a home reflecting safety and satisfaction. It was possible now to pause, and in the few hours of new-found leisure time the man could create eye-catching decorated boxes, while his wife fashioned distinctive quilts and rugs. All gave an air of warmth and security to the home.

That there were solid roots, new-found satisfaction and pride of achievement can be verified in other ways. During 1851, the Ontario census records that most farms on the concessions and sideroads had log houses; ten years later the vast majority had been replaced by storey-and-a-half frame houses with a living room. In 1861, one farmer recorded with a certain pride that in his cellar were two hogsheads of pork and two of beef, that in the previous year he had harvested seventy-five bushels of potatoes, two hundred and sixty-five of wheat and two hundred and forty of oats. He had three cows, eight steers, five sheep, two horses and two oxen. His wife had made twenty-

eight yards of homespun, two hundred pounds of butter and one hundred of cheese. Life was good! His record was a visible reassurance that he was, in fact, living the good life, just as the folk objects that decorated his house proclaimed his joy at success.

A more graphic expression of the same attitude may be seen in the county atlases that chronicled southern Ontario in the 1870s. Each detailed early settlement in the area, and included pictures of the patriarchs who made it all possible and of the fine new houses and municipal buildings that added distinction to the fine land. The exteriors of the houses were enhanced with trim flower beds, and their interiors were sprinkled with eye-catching folk art.

Quebec has a spirit and roots which are quite dissimilar to those of Ontario. This is partly due to the ancient Quebecois adherence to the Roman Catholic religion. Louiseville, in Maskinonge County, had had a mission church since 1714 when St. Anthony was chosen as the local patron saint. Each Sunday morning, the local habitant looked up to see the metal cock (No. 1) on the church spire, the same traditional action that took place in many other villages. The cock symbolized Peter's betrayal and reminded them of the obligations to God which had long been an integral part of their lives. This and similar simple objects are traditional art forms that conform more precisely to the old European definition that such art is rooted in beliefs passed on from generation to generation.

It is the habitant's ties to church and family held through the years which have isolated him from the frenetic North American spirit. He has been a simple man in the best sense of the word. When he passed his time in whittling, the contemplative side of his nature turned to carving figures of Christ on the Cross (No. 8). He knew little of anatomical detail, but he had a great will to make a truly symbolic figure. There is strength, even if unskilled, in the massive cross and rugged body of this example from the collection. This particular figure has been painted white as a symbol of Christian purity. In a more light-hearted moment, a Quebecois carver might turn to the making of moulds for the sugar harvest. Trees were tapped at Easter, so he carved his moulds in the forms of crosses, cocks, hearts, houses and even the parish church; these sculpted forms added eye appeal when the cakes of maple sugar were stored for home use or displayed for sale in the market.

The sterner religious side of the French Canadian nature is balanced by his natural exuberance and joy of living, all of which is portrayed in very personal and whimsical artistic ways. For example, he decorates his game board (No. 32) with odds and ends of colours left after the walls and floors in the home have been painted. Another such man was the carver Oscar Heon of Three Rivers who turned this balance into little figurines. His "The Notary Walking His Dog" (No. 95) is quaintly comical; that the dog closely resembles a polar bear is an additional virtue. The ancient figure carving tradition may have deteriorated into making rather bland figurines for the tourist trade, but men living far down the south shore of the St. Lawrence at Saint Jean Port Joli at the turn of the century bore no relationship to the souvenir maker. In that village, figure carving became infectious. One whittler visited the circus, the epitome of fantasy. He came home and carved a circus master with his high silk hat, broad shoulders and close fitting coat and put beside him his cocky little pony dutifully waiting to begin the act (No. 36).

Like the circus master and his pony, the carvings in the Price Collection are no literal transcription of reality; features are accentuated, others are eliminated, here and there distortion appears. The eye is jolted into recognizing a magnificent if humble plastic form which has transformed simple things into works of art.

The tracing of relationships between man's nature, his roots in the life he leads, and their expression in works of folk art can be extended to the Atlantic seaboard. Here, there are wide beaches and solitary intruders wandering in open spaces with wild creatures. Indians made decoys from bundles of reeds to catch fowl in prehistoric times. Europeans hunting in nineteenth century Canada created a carved decoy industry of great proportions. The decoy is a direct link between man and the wild, but there are two kinds. Some are fashioned to lure geese, ducks and other shore birds, they are devoid of love and appropriate only for use by hunters who kill for gain. Yet there are Prince Edward Islanders whose carved decoys speak of a passionate love and understanding of wild creatures and their essential nature. They leisurely fashioned decoys during long winter days when weather isolated them from the mainland and when there was time to savor memories of walks in their quiet island home.

Their carving reaches its greatest potential in the Canada goose. An Alberton carver speaks of a love affair with the noble bird when he emphasizes the long sweep of its extended neck (No. 65). Another carver seizes on the rhythmical circular motion of the bird's ruffled feathers (No. 63) when it senses danger and glances back for reassurance from the flock; this must be one of Canada's finest bird decoys. One among the crew made a little owl (No. 76). Its austerity is remarkable. It is a simple, direct carving with head and body emerging from the wooden block in crude planes, yet it embodies a haunting, evocative beauty. Surely there is a Walt Whitman nature in the men who made these decoys, since they clearly reflect carvers who are completely attuned to nature and the wild. They could be carved only by men in quiet places. The gesture of inner beauty in these objects is the same gesture expressed by Michelangelo in the slow expressive lines of awakening "Dawn" in the Medici Chapel of Florence. The immortal artist, of course, works in the great academic tradition, and the nameless little men in the humbler places speak in the humbler voices of the folk artist. Each has its own value, each its own beauty.

The folk carving tradition is as alive today as it was a century ago. It still retains qualities of feeling that made the art great in the past. The Price Collection is rich in contemporary models. Curiously, the majority of these express the love and satisfaction with which the farmer tills the soil and reaps the harvest. Mr. G. Stiles of Albert County in New Brunswick has spent his elderly years creating in miniature the farm implements he has known over his long life. Oxen pulling a load of grain is such a model (No. 87); his horses pulling a manure spreader (No. 88) must be one of the most earthy subjects in all Canadian folk art. Stiles' work closely parallels that of Ivan Law of Oshawa. Mr. Law had learned about good farming at the Ontario Agricultural College in his youth; he tilled the land north of Lake Ontario. As an old man he made models; eight horses pulling a wagon (No. 86) is his triumph, and it shows the same satisfaction with a good

life as earlier pieces.

There are those contemporary folk artists who simply want to make things. J. Seton Tompkins of the rural village of Singhampton in Ontario had worked with automobiles and been a service station operator all his life. He is a compulsive putterer, and in his retirement he has continued a life-long habit of recycling discarded things he found laying around. Ancient lawn chairs fastened together became the sculptor's armature for plastered and painted figures of a horse and trainer (No. 99). In more massive dimensions, his sculpted pair echoes the sentiments of the circus carver from Saint Jean Port Joli.

Tompkins also made smaller forms, such as the carved dog with a treed cat arching its back while sitting on a pole and spitting at its tormentor (No. 97). These figures are as slick and streamlined as the automobiles and metallic hood ornaments with which he had worked all his life.

An Acadian from Dieppe, New Brunswick, Art Gallant carved Zsa Zsa Gabor looking out from a television screen (No. 90), as well as K. C. Irving, the touted industrial tycoon of Gallant's province (No. 89). Television is his link with the world, it supplies his models, and the varnished finish with no trace of textural beauty reflects the sterile synthetic world of plastics that trickles into such places.

Much of this discussion has been about a utopian world which echoes rural satisfaction, a world of small bare-footed boys caressing soft dust in country lanes and of grandmothers with Christmas cakes on festive occasions. But even this world has its frustrated, and out of their frustration emerges another strain of folk art. Two such men of particular note whose works are represented in the Price Collection are Patrick O'Connor and George Cockayne. O'Connor lived at Bob's Lake in Frontenac County where the harsh Laurentian shield dips down to make that part of eastern Ontario unproductive. Nature robbed him of bountiful harvests, but he carved little wooden heads with bulging eyes (No. 80) which have the air of Pre-Columbian sacrificial figures. He also made a strange little creature that has a pink plastic comb for teeth (No. 83). By contrast, a little carving of a nun and the symbolism in a little red rooster (No. 81) may have originated in his Irish Catholic upbringing.

George Cockayne is a more flamboyant man. Raised as an orphan boy in England, he came to Canada during the Great Depression to work in the woods until he was able to buy a farm. Finally, he saved seven hundred dollars, bought his bit of land and lived half starving for two years until things improved slightly. He had learned to carve as a lad by the seaside, and he began to make things in his loneliness. *Beware the Yellow Band* is a grotesque figure of a man and a crawling snake (No. 101). The man's sneering mouth, the garish colours, give this figure a powerful mocking air. Cockayne never married, and one wonders whether the title might be a double entendre for marriage. At any rate, *The Yellow Band* is certainly the product of a lonely soul. In it Cockayne continues the folk art tradition, but his contemporary works reflect a very different mood than the peace and satisfaction so apparent in many earlier pieces.

It is perhaps appropriate to take a final look at a group of articles drawn from all five provinces, each of which serves a similar function and each of which reflects the spirit of the little places. Butter stamps were universally used in Canada, and they were nearly always made of wood. There were stamps of abstract design and others picturing farm animals, squirrels, acorns and clusters of cherries. The small ones decorated individual pats of salted butter put by the plate on festive or anniversary occasions when family, relatives and friends met together. They added an "air" to the table. Some were made by carvers who used such ancient symbolic designs as the Basque cross, the six-pointed star, or the tree of life which was traditional among the Pennsylvania-Germans (Nos. 24-27). Some could be bought from the T. Eaton Company catalogue in 1893 when a little individual print of a lamb cost eight cents, a half pound print, eighteen cents, and a pound print, twenty-five cents. The larger prints adorned the communal butter plate or were arresting when the country women sold their butter in town markets in much the same way as the appealingly shaped sugar moulds were used in Quebec. Many prints used in English-speaking Canada were the products of wood-turning artisans living along village streets. They were really cottage craftsmen whose work was so attuned to the simple living of their neighbours that the commercial aspects faded away.

It was this same merging of the craftsmen's product with the spirit of his neighbours that produced the tinsmith's tole ware, the village weaver's attractively patterned coverlets, or the potter's crocks decorated with exotic animals (No. 19). Still, among the butter stamps from Quebec is one quite unique specimen made with the whittler's knife (No. 23). On one side is a heart, on the other a stylized pine tree. Both are traditional symbolic designs dictated by folk custom. This individually made stamp was found in isolated Ile Aux Coudres from which come magnificent coverlets that are made only by habitants of that area. The print and the coverlets share common symbolic elements.

The Price Collection of Folk Art is a visual essay in Canadian self-revelation. It exposes diverse roots out of which this country has emerged. Ponder the meanings of the decorative touches that enliven the carvings, rugs, game boards and all the little things gathered here. It makes a graphic picture. It is a panorama of people drawn from many backgrounds, with diverse cultural heritages in which they still retain a sense of pride, of varied religions and many basic moods and natures. It demonstrates how these varied sources unite in roots that spring from the elemental nature of human existence, whether from the soil or the sea. These folk objects are expressions of a people with simple honesty and good will, rugged as the great trees of the forest, and with the uncomplicated approach to life of basic things. They have a justifiable sense of pride in achievement. They are folk who take quiet delight in the innate beauty that rests in simple hearts. The making of this collection has been an on-going activity for Dr. and Mrs. Price. It promises to provide in the future, as it has in the past, an excitement in finding new and lovely things. Each discovery will open new avenues for thought and contemplation, demonstrating yet other facets of the Canadian identity.

J. Russell Harper
Alexandria, Ontario

*This rakish, almost malevolent bird has a
magnificent surface. It came from the earliest chapel
in Louiseville which was torn down in 1913.*

1
Weathercock
Artist unknown
Louiseville, Quebec
Formed metal, paint over tar
Early 18th century
48 x 86 cms.

2
Weathercock
Artist unknown
Quebec
Formed metal, painted
Mid-19th century
50 x 72 cms.

3
Chanteclêr
Artist unknown
Gaspé, Quebec
Formed metal, painted
Early 19th century
78 x 62 cms.

A very plump, fertile-looking bird.

4
Running Horse Weathervane
Artist unknown
North of Iroquois, Ontario
Sheet tin, reinforced with wrought iron
Ca. 1865
66 x 114 cms.

5
Rooster Weathervane
Artist unknown
Newmarket, Ontario
Cut sheet metal
Second half 19th century
60 x 76 cms.

*A proud tin rendition of
a most important domestic animal.*

*An unusually large, bold
Ontario rooster silhouette.*

6
Beaver Weathervane
Artist unknown
Omemee, Ontario
Formed tin, painted
Second half 19th century
40 x 83 cms.

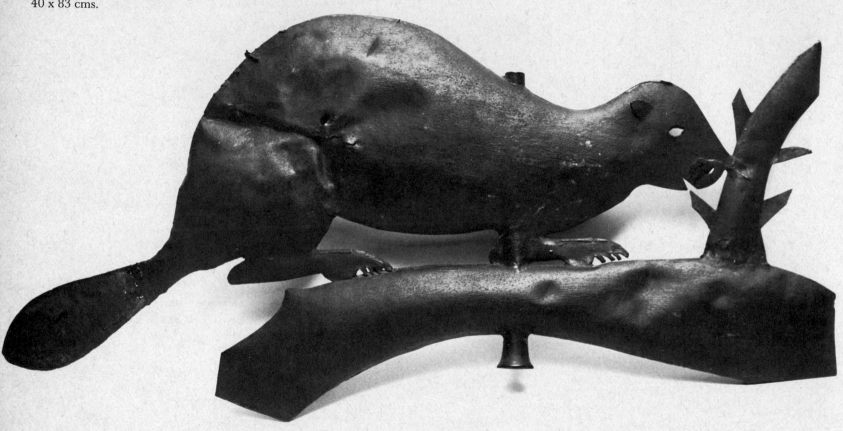

When this beaver was purchased,
        the owner reserved the right to make a pattern from it.
Today, just west of Omemee,
        the clone of this beaver is firmly ensconced on a barn roof.

*We have seen other crucifixes
in Quebec by the same artist.*

7
Crucifix
Artist unknown
Quebec
Carved, painted
wood (small forged nails)
Ca. 1800
63 x 41 cms.

8
Crucifix
Artist unknown
Quebec
Carved, painted wood
First half 20th century
60 x 25 cms.

*The earliest dated piece in our collection, this
oval box, which is similar to Palardy #557, is
in the so-called "Indian manner". It is signed
within (on the bottom) "Reine S ∴ Marsiere 1779."
Outside (on the bottom) it is signed "Reines ∴
Marsieres 1773." It is generally felt that
these boxes originated on the north shore of the
St. Lawrence between Three Rivers and Quebec City.*

9
Oval Wooden Box
By or for Reine S. Marsiere
Quebec, probably Port Neuf County
Wood, low relief carving on the lid, painted
1773
24 x 49 x 29 cms.

10
Sewing Box
Artist unknown
Maritime Provinces
Wood, joined with cut nails, painted
Mid-19th century
27 x 42 x 27 cms.

This box, with its boldly geometric paint job,
has a spindle inside that holds the spools, and
the thread exits through tiny holes at the apices
of the triangles on the face of the box.

11
Wall Shelf with Drawer
Artist unknown
Wilno, Ontario
Wood, joined, carved and grain painted
Ca. 1870
79 x 44 x 16 cms.

12
A Wall Box
Artist unknown
Quebec
Wood, joined, carved and painted
Mid-19th century
48 x 28.5 x 12 cms.

13
Sewing Box
Artist unknown
Lunenberg County, Nova Scotia
Wood, joined and painted, with cutouts
Second half 19th century
40 cms.

14
A Small Carved Chest
Artist unknown
Quebec
Wood, joined with forged nails;
low relief carving; painted
Early 19th century
42 x 61 x 42 cms.

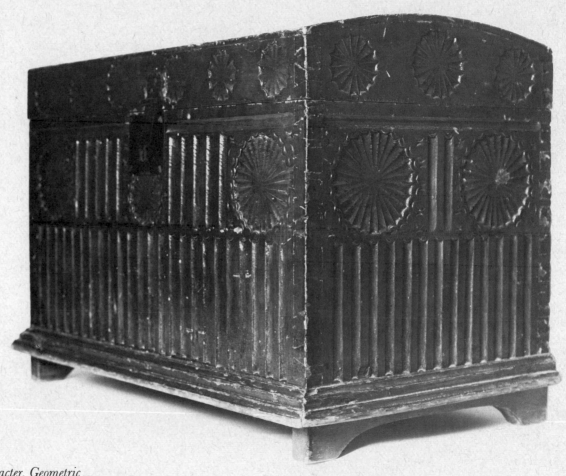

*This box has an almost gothic character. Geometric
motifs, such as these sunbursts, date from antiquity.
Originally having powerful symbolic meaning,
probably by the early 19th century they were
purely decorative. The lock is a late intrusion.*

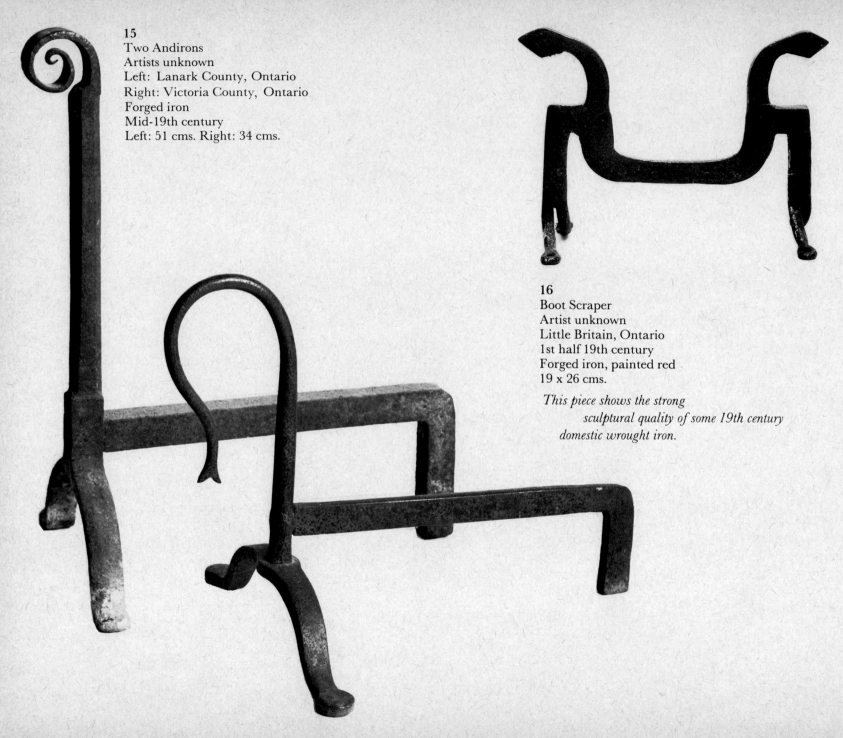

15
Two Andirons
Artists unknown
Left: Lanark County, Ontario
Right: Victoria County, Ontario
Forged iron
Mid-19th century
Left: 51 cms. Right: 34 cms.

16
Boot Scraper
Artist unknown
Little Britain, Ontario
1st half 19th century
Forged iron, painted red
19 x 26 cms.

*This piece shows the strong
    sculptural quality of some 19th century
domestic wrought iron.*

17
Four Wrought Iron Forks
Artists unknown
Top to bottom:
Port Perry, Ontario; Campbellford, Ontario;
Pickering, Ontario; Havelock, Ontario
Forged iron
Early 19th century
35 to 45 cms.

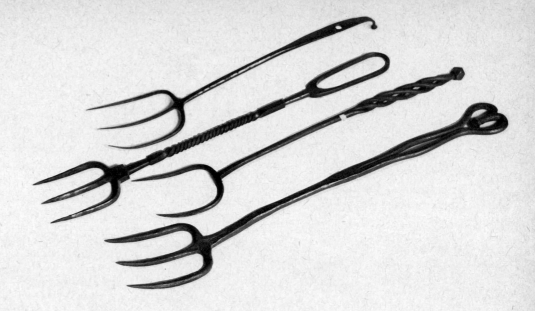

18
Three Wrought Iron Trivets
Artists unknown
Two outer pieces,
eastern Ontario; central piece, P.E.I.
Early 19th century
Forged iron
Left to right: 23, 18, and 14 cms.

*The heart motif lent itself
very well to the trivet form.
These are perhaps betrothal items.*

19
Three Stoneware Crocks
Left to right:
S. Skinner & Co., Picton, C. W.; Warner & Co.,
Toronto; S. Skinner & Co., Picton, C. W.
Stoneware, blue slip decoration
Mid-19th century
Left to right: 27, 35, 17 cms.

The central crock has most unusual decoration. The nature of the illustrated beast is obscure. We tend to think it looks most like a hyena, perhaps copied from a book of wild animals. We have seen a lion decoration, probably by the same hand, on an American crock by W. H. Farrar (1841-1857), Geddes, New York. See Antiques, Vol. CXIV, No. 1 (July, 1978), p. 42. This might suggest that the decorator was transient, moving from pottery to pottery.

20
Hackle
Artist unknown
Found in Waterloo County
Wood, decorated with a punch;
forged iron teeth
Late 18th century
63 x 16 cms.

*Said to be used to carry butter, it has the grease
stains to attest to this. Similar decorative motifs
are seen throughout eastern Canada in many media:
woodenware, textiles, decorated stoneware, etc.*

21
Cabbage Shredder
Artist unknown
Waterloo County
Cherrywood with a steel blade
Mid-19th century
76 x 17 cms.

22
Butterbox
Artist unknown
Quebec City area
Wood, decorated with low relief carving
Early 19th century
11.5 cms.

23
Four Butter Stamps
Artists unknown
Left to right:
Orangeville, Ontario; Ile Aux Coudres, P.Q.;
Kemptville, Ontario; Perth, Ontario
Carved wood
Early 19th century
Diameters, left to right: 12, 10, 11.5, 10.5 cms.

24
Butter Stamp
Artist unknown
Grimsby, Ontario
Carved wood
Early 19th century
13.5 cms.

25
Butter Stamp
Artist unknown
Port Hope, Ontario
Carved wood
Early 19th century
11 cms.

26
Butter Stamp
Artist unknown
Lanark, Ontario
Carved wood
Early 19th century
12 cms.

27
Butter Stamp
Artist unknown
Bewdley, Ontario
Carved wood
Early 19th century
10 cms.

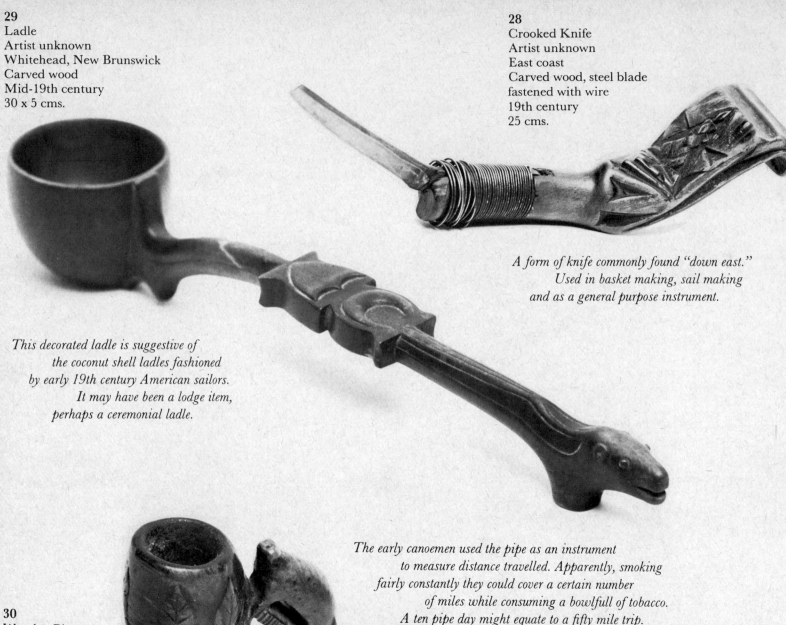

29
Ladle
Artist unknown
Whitehead, New Brunswick
Carved wood
Mid-19th century
30 x 5 cms.

28
Crooked Knife
Artist unknown
East coast
Carved wood, steel blade
fastened with wire
19th century
25 cms.

A form of knife commonly found "down east."
Used in basket making, sail making
and as a general purpose instrument.

This decorated ladle is suggestive of
the coconut shell ladles fashioned
by early 19th century American sailors.
It may have been a lodge item,
perhaps a ceremonial ladle.

30
Wooden Pipe
Artist unknown
Bewdley, Ontario
Carved maple
Early 19th century
10 x 5 cms.

The early canoemen used the pipe as an instrument
to measure distance travelled. Apparently, smoking
fairly constantly they could cover a certain number
of miles while consuming a bowlfull of tobacco.
A ten pipe day might equate to a fifty mile trip.

31
Four Walking Sticks
Artists unknown
Left to right:
Darlington Township, Ontario; Niagara Peninsula;
Belleville, Ontario; Niagara Peninsula
Carved wood
(the one on the extreme right has painted details)
Left to right:
Mid-19th century; early 20th century; mid-19th
century; second half 19th century
Left to right:
86, 80, 91, 94 cms.

The walking stick was a favourite product
of the whittler. Carved by many individuals
from all parts of the country, certain themes tend
to recur. The most common theme is that of
the snake entwining the stick. This is quite
probably a remembrance of the Biblical scene
of Moses in the desert and his staff that
became a snake. Certainly, such Biblical
themes were common in folk art.

32
Wooden Gameboard
Artist unknown
Quebec
Painted wood
Mid-19th century
60 x 65 cms.

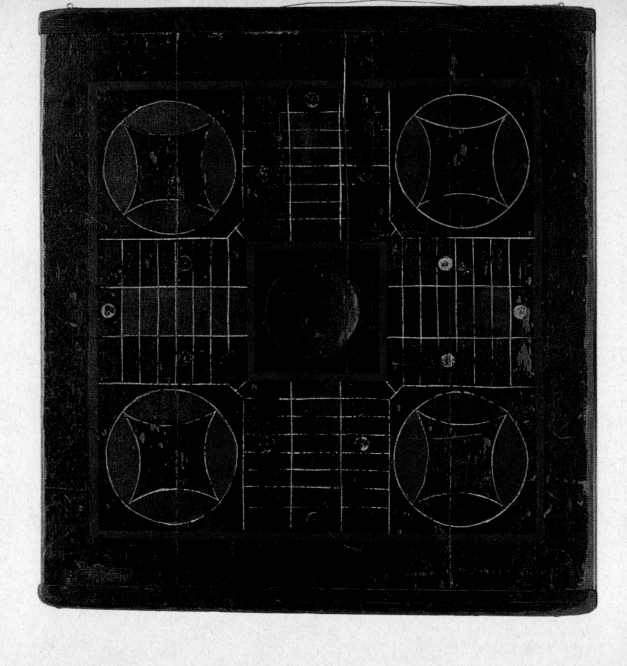

*This piece has much of the
        feeling of a nomadic oriental
rug. It is reversible, with
        parchesi on the pictured side
and checkers on the reverse.*

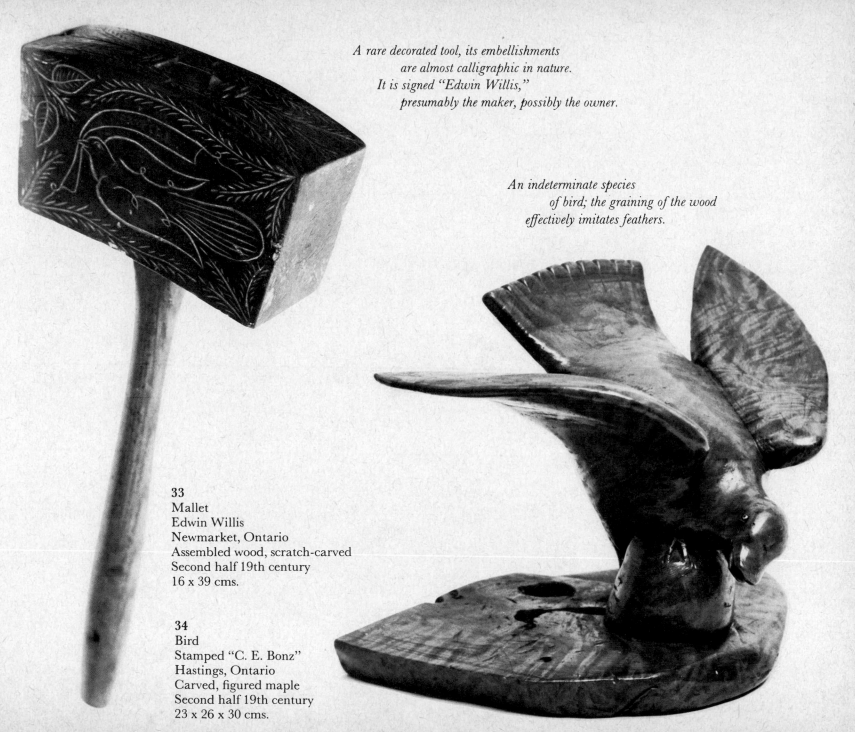

*A rare decorated tool, its embellishments
are almost calligraphic in nature.
It is signed "Edwin Willis,"
presumably the maker, possibly the owner.*

*An indeterminate species
of bird; the graining of the wood
effectively imitates feathers.*

33
Mallet
Edwin Willis
Newmarket, Ontario
Assembled wood, scratch-carved
Second half 19th century
16 x 39 cms.

34
Bird
Stamped "C. E. Bonz"
Hastings, Ontario
Carved, figured maple
Second half 19th century
23 x 26 x 30 cms.

41

35
Horse
Artist unknown
Maritime Provinces
Carved, painted wood
Late 19th century
35.5 x 37 cms.

42

36
Circus Master and Horse
Artist unknown
St. Jean Port Joli, Quebec
Carved, polychromed wood
Late 19th century
31 cms.

*Possibly, these two figures
were part of a larger set
of circus figures.*

37
Three Chickens
Artist unknown
Lac du deux Montagnes, Quebec
Carved wood and metal
Early 20th century
13 x 29 cms.

38
Rocking Horse
Silas Brokenshire
Fenelon Falls, Ontario
Carved, painted wood; cut nails
1890
69, 117, 38 cms.

This horse was made about 1890 by Silas Brokenshire,
a pump-maker from Fenelon Falls, Ontario, for his
son, Foster. A powerful beast, this is the sort of
thing one would expect from a man whose days were
spent turning wooden pumps. It is a good example
of the artisan or craftsman tradition
from which folk art springs.

39
"Souvenir de L'heureuse famille Francois Mailhot"
Artist unknown
Quebec
Oil on canvas
Juillet, 1896
77 x 116 cms.

40
A Pair of Pigeons
Artist unknown
Fisher's Glen, Norfolk County, Ontario
Oil on canvas
Mid-19th century
33 x 26 cms.

These were painted by an artist
of some skill, probably after a book
of prints, a common exercise for
the self-taught artist.

41
Portrait of a Cat
Artist unknown
Eastern Ontario (Kingston area)
Oil on artist's board
Second half 19th century
47 x 31.5 cms.

42
Birds
Artist unknown
Berlin (Kitchener), Ontario
Tinsel picture
1872
58 x 53 cms.

*Replete with symbolism
so typical of the
Pennsylvania-Germans
who first settled the area.*

43
Peacocks
Artist unknown
Western Ontario (Whiarton area)
Tinsel picture
Ca. 1850
47 x 90 cms.

*Probably a copy of a print;
we have encountered other pictures
with nearly identical content.*

44
Portrait of a Girl and Her Dog
Artist unknown
Eastern Townships, Quebec
Graphite, water colour, or pastel
Second half 19th century
53 x 43 cms.

45
Canoeing Scene
Mr. Gandier
Lindsay, Ontario
Wooden bas relief plaque
1920
35 x 54 cms.

46
The Village of Iroquois, "Scenes of Our School Days"
Herbert Jube
Iroquois, Ontario
Oil paint on cardboard
1957
53 x 71 cms.

47
Tyrone Mill
Gloria Thornbeck
Tyrone, Ontario
Oil paint on masonite
Early 1960s
41.5 x 83 cms.

48
Hooked Mat
Mrs. Crozier
Lennox and Addington
County, Ontario
Wool
Early 1900s
91 x 97 cms.

The rooster
was traced
from a weathervane
on the Crozier's barn
and the odd feet
(which look like a pair
of rubber gloves)
were added by
the artist.

49
Hooked Mat
Artist unknown
Ontario County
Cotton and wool
Late 19th century
127 x 66 cms.

This was a printed pattern or done
after a printed pattern.
However, the unusual, human, Hitler-like
face on the lion demonstrates the liberties
taken by the more artistic hookers.

50
Hooked Mat
Artist unknown
Quebec
Cotton
Early 1900s
102 x 65 cms.

It is uncertain whether
the dog cannot get into
the house or is not allowed
— probably both.

51
Hooked Mat
Florence Graham
Purple Hill, Ontario
Cotton
1930
100 x 65 cms.

52
Hooked Mat
Flora Christie
Manchester, Ontario
Wool
1950
96 x 61 cms.

53
Hooked Mat
Flora Christie
Manchester, Ontario
Wool
1950
91 x 58 cms.

54
Basket and Noonday Lily Quilt
Artist unknown
Sawyerville, Quebec
Pieced cotton
Second half 19th century
216 x 210 cms.

55
Rose of Sharon Quilt
Mrs. Wilson
Nestleton, Cartwright Township, Ontario
Cotton appliqué
Third quarter 19th century
190 x 180 cms.

56
Pieced and Appliquéd Quilt Top
Artist unknown
Niagara Peninsula
Cotton
Third quarter 19th century
220 x 208 cms.

57
Windmill and Diamond Square Quilt
Edith May Prout
Zephyr, Ontario
Homespun wool
Fourth quarter 19th century
220 x 160 cms.

58
Beaver Trade Sign
Artist unknown
Stalter's Music Store, Oshawa, Ontario
Carved, painted wood
Late 19th or early 20th century
33 x 75 cms.

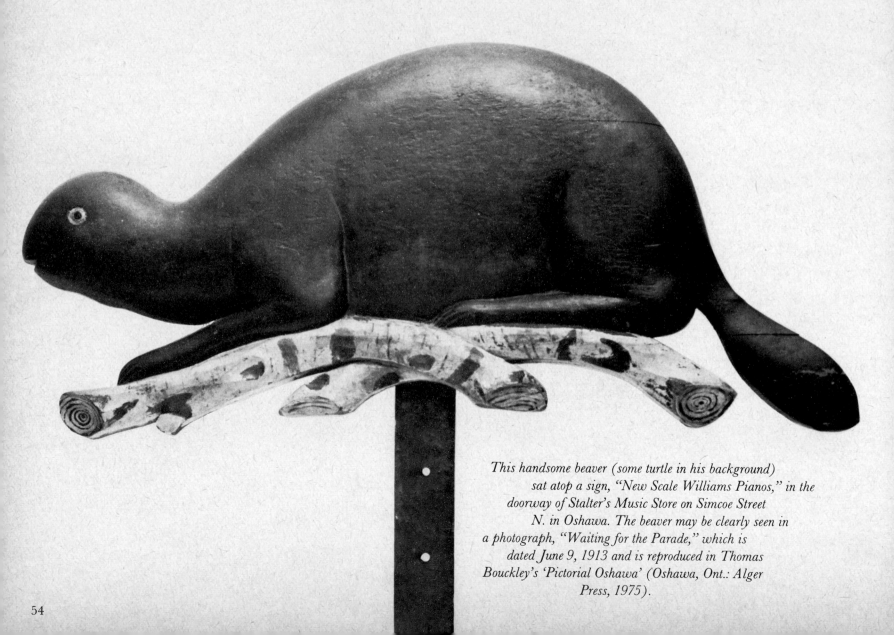

*This handsome beaver (some turtle in his background)
sat atop a sign, "New Scale Williams Pianos," in the
doorway of Stalter's Music Store on Simcoe Street
N. in Oshawa. The beaver may be clearly seen in
a photograph, "Waiting for the Parade," which is
dated June 9, 1913 and is reproduced in Thomas
Bouckley's 'Pictorial Oshawa' (Oshawa, Ont.: Alger
Press, 1975).*

59
The Bonfield Barber Shop
Artist unknown
Bonfield, Ontario
Carved wood, unpainted, mounted on plywood
1930s
24 x 38 x 31 cms.

*During the Depression years,
this vignette in wood
sat in the window of a barber shop
in Bonfield, Ontario,
a small town near North Bay.*

61
Counter-Top Cigar Store Indian
Artist unknown
Found at Pictou, Nova Scotia
Carved, painted wood
Second half 19th century
58 cms.

*Small trade figures
such as this one stood
inside the tobacco shops
on the counter.*

*This trade figure is known
to have graced the Riley Tobacco Company
in Charlottetown from
as early as 1873.*

60
Alice, the Cigar Store Indian Maiden
Artist Unknown
Found in Charlottetown, P. E. I.
Carved, painted wood
Second half 19th century
155 cms. (excluding base)

62
Canada Goose Decoy
Artist unknown (possibly G. & J. Warin)
Toronto area
Carved, painted wood (hollow body)
Late 19th century
61 cms.

Very similar to the decoys made and signed by
G. & J. Warin (1873-1904). See Bernard W.
Crandell, "The Warins of Toronto," 'North American
Decoys' (Spring, 1975), pp. 6-11.

63
Preening Goose Decoy
George Skerry
Lot 16, Prince Edward Island
Carved wood (charring and white paint)
Early 20th century
51 cms.

This graceful, flowing, stick-up decoy, blackened by charring, was apparently made as one of a kind.

64
Feeding Goose Decoy
Artist unknown
Nova Scotia
Carved wood, painted, hollow body
Ca. 1900
67 cms.

65
Reaching Goose Decoy
Artist unknown
P. E. I.
Carved, painted wood
Late 19th century
81 cms.

66
Two Hooded Merganser Drake Decoys
Artist unknown
Prescott, Ontario
Carved, painted wood
Mid-20th century
26 cms.

67
Black Duck ("Guzzler") Decoy
Angus Lake
West Lake, Ontario
Carved, painted wood
Ca. 1900
53 cms.

A powerful, greedy black duck who is reaching
for food or possibly driving away a rival. Angus
Lake was the postmaster of West Lake, Ontario,
and was a prolific decoy carver.

Three of a rig of very sturdy,
well-painted black ducks.

68
Three Black Duck Decoys
Artist unknown
Foxboro, Ontario
Carved, painted wood
First half 20th century
39 cms.

69
A Pair of Hooded Merganser Drake Decoys
Artist unknown
Perth Road Village, Ontario
Carved, painted wood
Late 19th century
29 cms.

*Possibly the faceted surfaces were the carver's
way of eliminating glare, a common problem
with decoys. In any event, the total effect
makes for a most pleasing and handsome pair
of male Hooded Mergansers.*

70
Two Blue-Winged Teal Decoys
William Ellis
Whitby, Ontario
Carved, painted wood
Mid-1930s
Female: 31 cms. Male: 34 cms.

71
Canvas Back Drake Decoy
W. Avis
Frenchman's Bay, Ontario
Carved, painted wood (hollow)
Early 20th century
40 cms.

72
Two White-Winged Scoter Decoys
Lawrence Davis
Toronto, Ontario
Carved, painted wood
Ca. 1930
38 cms.

These two sea ducks were carved in the early 1930s
  by Lawrence Davis of Toronto. At the time, he was
working as a carpenter for the T. Eaton Company.
        During these early Depression years, he would
  supplement his income by carving working birds.
        Lawrence could carve from dusk to dawn and then
carry twelve birds, paint still wet, to work with
        him. For each one he was given sixty-five cents.
An order for four dozen of these birds came in
        from the Moncton, New Brunswick, store, and he
        undertook to make them. He has been told on
good authority that some of this four dozen rig
        were found much later in a boathouse in Iceland.

73
Two Heron Decoys
Lawrence Davis
Found on Scugog Island
Carved, painted wood, glass eyes, iron legs
1930
84 cms.

74
Two Shorebird Decoys
Artist unknown
Prince Edward Island
Carved, painted wood
Second half 19th century
Left: 21 cms. Right: 24 cms.

75
Crow Decoy
Artist unknown
Brighton, Ontario
Laminated wood,
carved and painted,
wire legs, glass eyes
First half 20th century
48 cms.

When coupled with a crow call,
  this bold decoy probably lured
many an unsuspecting crow
    to an early demise.

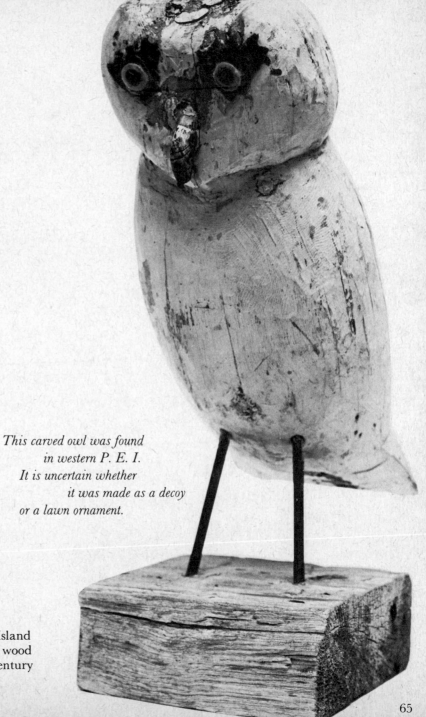

This carved owl was found
    in western P. E. I.
It is uncertain whether
      it was made as a decoy
or a lawn ornament.

76
Owl
Artist unknown
Prince Edward Island
Carved, painted wood
First half 19th century
37 cms.

*This is a long, tall, authoritarian
figure whose arms would spin with the wind,
one is almost tempted to say directing traffic.*

77
Policeman Whirlygig
Artist unknown
Elgin, Ontario
Carved, painted wood
Late 19th century
68 cms.

78
Cat
Artist unknown
Belleville, Ontario
Carved, painted wood, laminated
Early 20th century
60 cms.

*In Britain, apparently, cat models are left in
berry patches to keep the birds away. This cat
shows evidence of weathering and many have been
used for this purpose, or it may just have been
intended as a yard ornament.*

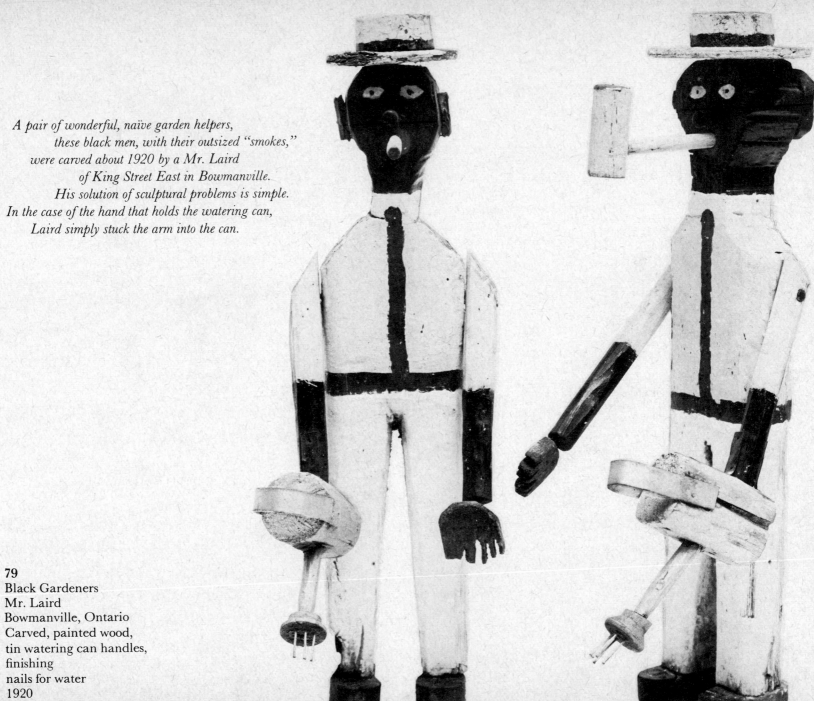

A pair of wonderful, naïve garden helpers,
*   these black men, with their outsized "smokes,"*
were carved about 1920 by a Mr. Laird
*   of King Street East in Bowmanville.*
*   His solution of sculptural problems is simple.*
In the case of the hand that holds the watering can,
Laird simply stuck the arm into the can.

79
Black Gardeners
Mr. Laird
Bowmanville, Ontario
Carved, painted wood,
tin watering can handles,
finishing
nails for water
1920
45 cms.

80
Seven Carved Heads
Patrick O'Connor
Bob's Lake, Ontario
Carved wood, some painted
First half 20th century
5 to 9 cms.

*Shown here are some of a great number of carvings
by Patrick O'Connor of Bob's Lake, Ontario.
Apparently, he was born in the late 19th century,
for he died in his seventies in 1960.
O'Connor farmed in the limestone country in
northwest Frontenac County — subsistence farming.
At present, we have been able to find out
relatively little about this man.
That he was a compulsive whittler is apparent, for
we have seen seventy to eighty of his carvings.*

81
Rooster
Patrick O'Connor
Bob's Lake, Ontario
Carved, painted wood
First half 20th century
14 x 14 cms.

83
Baboon (?)
Patrick O'Connor
Bob's Lake, Ontario
Carved wood, coconut shell,
plastic teeth
First half 20th century
14.5 x 9 cms.

82
Exotic Bird
Patrick O'Connor
Bob's Lake, Ontario
Carved, painted wood
Early 20th century
18 cms.

84
"Clip Short," Blacksmith
Ivan Law
Oshawa, Ontario
Carved, polychromed wood
1972
16 cms.

85
Lion, Lioness and Cubs
Ivan Law
Oshawa, Ontario
Carved, painted wood
March, 1973
10 x 25 x 8 cms.

*Clip Short was the blacksmith at Solina,
Ontario, early in the 20th century.*

86
Wagon with Driver and Eight Horse Team
Ivan Law
Oshawa, Ontario
Carved, painted wood
1974
25 x 125 cms.

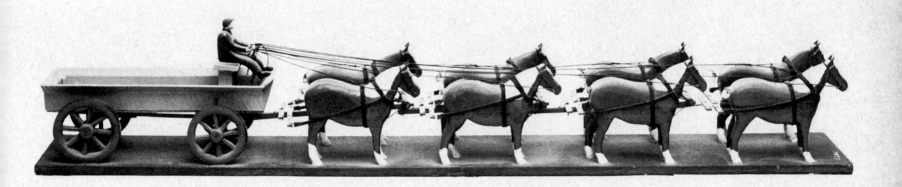

This figure, with its strong repetitive horses,
recalls fond memories of a country fair.

91
"Sea Crest"
Art Gallant
Dieppe, New Brunswick
Carved, painted wood and string
Ca. 1960
31 x 62 cms.

92
"Wrestlers"
Art Gallant
Dieppe, New Brunswick
Carved, painted and varnished wood
Ca. 1970
17 cms.

93
"The Lion — The Boss of the Forest"
Art Gallant
Dieppe, New Brunswick
Carved, varnished wood
Ca. 1973
23 x 32 cms.

The wrestlers and referee are
all carved from a single block of wood.
Mr. Gallant is fond of explaining his pieces
with stamped lettering,
just in case you missed the point.

94
Groundhog
Albert Hoto
Stromness, Ontario
Carved, stained wood
Early 1950s
44 x 20 x 20 cms.

95
"The Notary Walking His Dog"
Oscar Heon
Three Rivers, Quebec
Carved, painted wood
Mid-20th century
34 x 20 cms

*The little fellow was carved by Mr. Albert Hoto
of Stromness, Ontario, about 1950. Mr. Hoto
retired in the early 1950s, sold his farm and
hung out a shingle proclaiming himself an
"ornamental wood carver." He was evidently a
prodigious carver, often of life-sized figures.
Like this groundhog, many were intended as
lawn ornaments.*

76

96
Eagle and Fish
Billy Andrews
Bradford, Ontario
Carved, painted wood
1974
40 x 76 x 35 cms.

*A dejected looking eagle
    sadly eyeing what looks like a fish
straight from the freezer.*

97
Cat on a Post with Dog
J. Seton Tompkins
Singhampton, Ontario
Carved, painted wood
September, 1976
42 x 24 cms.

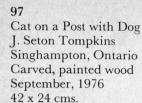

98
Bull and Matador
J. Seton Tompkins
Singhampton, Ontario
Carved, painted wood
1976
15 x 45 cms.

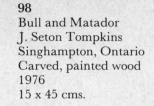

*Mr. Tompkins was a spectator
at the only bull fight ever held in Canada,
at the Lindsay, Ontario, Fall Fair in the early 1950s.*

*J. Seton Tompkins was born in the Singhampton area
in 1899 and ran an Esso Service Station there
until 1967. Shortly after his retirement he
began to create sculptural pieces using
various techniques. His finishes are highly polished
much like the automobiles he worked with for
over fifty years. Either of these animals could
be a hood ornament.*

100
Groom and Horse
J. Seton Tompkins
Singhampton, Ontario
Groom: carved, painted wood
Horse: Welded metal,
mesh and stucco
1968
100 x 146 cms.

99
Circus Master and Rearing Horse
J. Seton Tompkins
Singhampton, Ontario
Welded metal, mesh and stucco;
carved wood — painted
1975
Master: 140 cms. Horse 163 cms.

101
"Beware the Yellow Band"
George Cockayne
Madoc, Ontario
Carved, polychromed wood
1975
150 cms.

102
Peewee
George Cockayne
Prince Edward County, Ontario
Carved, polychromed wood
with shotgun shells
1932
30 x 28 cms.

*This low relief carved shotgun shell holder
        was done while Mr. Cockayne was still living
in Prince Edward County.
        It apparently depicts him, his dog
and his pet ferret, Peewee, hunting rabbits.*

103
"The Raja"
George Cockayne
Madoc, Ontario
Carved, polychromed wood
1976
40 cms.

During the winters, Mr. Cockayne worked
in lumbering camps both in Ontario and British
Columbia, and it was in these camps that he
started carving. Initially, his carvings were
of his fellow workers or the camp boss. He
found he could sell these pieces for a dollar —
at that time a good day's wages. More recently,
his models have been derived from his reading.
Cockayne is an avid magazine reader. As well, he
feels compelled to make "something out of nothing,"
with the result that most of his pieces have been
made from scraps and leftovers. Everything he
makes has to be useful, although admittedly
the uses are somewhat obscure. The Yellow Band,
for example: he felt that it could stand in the
foyer of a large house, and the butler could
place the callers' cards on the tray.

Bibliography

Ames, Kenneth L. *Beyond Necessity: Art in the Folk Tradition.* New York: W. W. Norton & Co., Inc., 1977.

Barbeau, Marius. *I Have Seen Quebec.* Toronto: The Macmillan Company of Canada, Ltd., 1957.

Barber, Joel. *Wildfowl Decoys.* New York: Dover Publications Inc., 1954.

Bishop, Robert. *American Folk Sculpture.* New York: E. P. Dutton and Company, Inc., 1974.

Bouckley, Thomas. *Pictorial Oshawa.* Oshawa: The Alger Press Ltd., 1975.

Burnham, Harold B., and Dorothy K. Burnham. *Keep Me Warm One Night.* Toronto: University of Toronto Press, 1972.

Cheever, Byron, and Maureen Cheever. *Mason Decoys.* Herber City, Utah: Hillcrest Publications, Inc., 1974.

Collard, Elizabeth. *Nineteenth Century Pottery and Porcelain in Canada.* Montreal: McGill University Press, 1967.

Crandell, Bernard W. "The Warins of Toronto." *North American Decoys* (Spring, 1975), pp. 6-11.

Cuisenier, Jean. *French Folk Art.* New York: Kodansha International Ltd., 1977.

Earnest, Adele. *The Art of the Decoy: American Bird Carvings.* New York: Clarkson N. Potter, Inc., 1965.

Evans, Harold B. "Brownheads." *North American Decoys* (Spring, 1975), pp. 14-16.

Fales, Dean A., Jr. *American Painted Furniture, 1660-1880.* New York: E. P. Dutton and Company, Inc., 1972.

Harper, J. Russell. *Painting in Canada.* Toronto: University of Toronto Press, 1966.

Harper, J. Russell. *People's Art: Naïve Art in Canada.* Ottawa: The National Gallery of Canada, 1973.

Harper, J. Russell. *A People's Art: Primitive, Naïve, Provincial and Folk Painting in Canada.* Toronto: University of Toronto Press, 1974.

Hemphill, Herbert W., Jr., and Julia Weissman. *Twentieth-Century American Folk Art and Artists.* New York: E. P. Dutton and Company, Inc., 1974.

Hornung, Clarence P. *Treasury of American Design.* 2 Vols. New York: Harry N. Abrams, Inc., 1950.

Horwitz, Elinor Lander. *Contemporary American Folk Artists.* Philadelphia: J. B. Lippincott Company, 1975.

Ketchum, William C., Jr. *Early Potters and Potteries of New York State.* New York: Funk and Wagnalls, 1970.

Kopp, Joel, and Kate Kopp. *American Hooked and Sewn Rugs: Folk Art Underfoot.* New York: E. P. Dutton and Company, Inc., 1975.

Lipman, Jean, and Alice Winchester. *The Flowering of American Folk*

Art. New York: The Viking Press, 1974.

Mackey, William J., Jr. *American Bird Decoys.* New York: Bonanza Books, 1965.

The Magazine Antiques. Advertisement. Vol. CXIV, No. 1 (July, 1978), p. 42.

Michigan Folk Art: Its Beginnings to 1941. East Lansing, Michigan: Michigan State University Board of Trustees, 1976.

Owens, Richard M., et al. *American Denim.* New York: Harry N. Abrams, Inc., 1975.

Pain, Howard. *The Heritage of Upper Canadian Furniture: A Study in the Survival of Formal and Vernacular Styles from Britain, America and Europe, 1780-1900.* Toronto: Van Nostrand Rheinhold, Ltd., 1978.

Palardy, Jean. *The Early Furniture of French Canada.* Toronto: Macmillan of Canada, 1965.

Pendergast, A. W., and W. Porter Ware. *Cigar Store Figures in American Folk Art.* Chicago: Lightner Publishing Corporation, 1953.

Pinto, Edward H. *Treen and Other Wooden Bygones.* London: G. Bell & Sons, 1969.

Price, Ralph. "Ontario Decoys as Folk Art." *Circa 76,* Vol. 1, No. 9 (n. d.), pp. 14-16.

Safford, Carleton L., and Robert Bishop. *America's Quilts and Coverlets.* New York: E. P. Dutton and Company, Inc., 1972.

Séguin, Robert-Lionel. *Les Jouets Anciens Du Québec.* Ottawa: Les Editions Leméac Inc., 1969.

Shackleton, Philip. *The Furniture of Old Ontario.* Toronto: Macmillan of Canada, 1973.

Stoudt, John Joseph. *Early Pennsylvania Arts and Crafts.* New York: A. S. Barnes & Company, Inc., 1964.

Webster, Donald. *Early Canadian Pottery.* Toronto: McClelland and Stewart, Ltd., 1971.

Index ॐ

Design and Photography/Howard Pain

Textile Photography/Blake McKendry

Editorial Consultant/James T. Wills

Typesetting/Howarth & Smith Limited

Printing/Herzig Somerville Limited

This book was produced in Canada